PROTOCOL S

"Happiness is like a butterfly,
Which when pursued, is always just beyond your grasp,
But which,
If you sit down quietly,
May alight upon you"

Author Unknown

I believe that happiness is an Art.

And every form of Art is actually an expression of a particular skill, a very unique expression of each artist. Therefore, happiness is as unique in its individual meaning as the artist himself or herself.

But if happiness is a skill, then like all skills it can be studied, learnt and improved. Levels of individual happiness can go up or down, and like any other skill, it needs a bit of polishing and nourishing from time to time.

The main objective of this book is to raise the baseline of your current level of happiness. Once this is accomplished, you can build on it and nurture it.

Lesson number one is the **'Art of Being Yo**u', the most important kind of Art as there is no other person like you in the whole world.

You are unquestionably unique and you need to start appreciate being you. But in order to appreciate yourself, you need to first acknowledge who you really are.
Not, who you *think* you are, but who you really are.

You probably heard a saying that 'happiness is in your gut' or 'you are what you eat'.
Personally, I could not agree more so I decided to cover this topic in my lesson number two – **'The Art of Tafelspitz'**.

We will tidy our space and discover the **'Art of Enlightened Minimalism'**, so you can focus more on living and being rather than of having. This is Art lesson number three for you.

In lesson four, we will stop following crowds like sheep or lemurs and admit that it is perfectly okay to take a break from social influencers and other pretenders.

We will perfect the **'Art of Doing Nothing'**, because, honestly, you do not need to have plans for every weekend of the year.

We will come back to the 'Art of Being You' with a clear mind and space around you, with a healthy, nourished body and some free time to finally 'have a go' at being you.

Have you ever wondered why artist paint several copies of the same painting?

Protocol
Of
The Art of Happiness

Malgorzata Pasko-Szczech

For my son Maximillian
And
In loving memory of my grandmother Zofia Wanic

CONTENTS

ACKNOWLEDGMENTS

All photos are property of the author.

All stated opinions along with relevant references represent personal opinions of the author.

THE ART OF BEING YOU – *THE MOST IMPORTANT KIND OF ART*

"If I want to be free, I've got to be me…

…Not the me you think I should be, not the me my wife thinks I should be, not the me I think my kids think I should be.

If I want to be free, I've got to be me so I better know who me is."

Bill Gove

The question came unexpectedly as it had no relevance, not even remote, to the post I applied for:

- *'If you had a chance to be born as someone else, who would you like to be and why? Think of a person you admire and are inspired by.'*

My reply was equally unexpected, I suspect:

'I could think of two women at this moment who have either shaped my life or contributed in some ways to me being the kind of person I am today.

My first choice would always be my grandmother Zofia Wanic, who played a crucial part in my upbringing after my father's tragic death.
To this day, I see and analyze the world largely through her eyes.

I never met my second choice – Simone Veil [1], who was a prominent French politician, French Minister of Healthcare and who became the first female President of the European Parliament.
I read her books twice and I know I am going to read them again.

Their lives were also tragic.

Zofia lost most of her family during WW II, her infant son died shortly after he was born and her whole life was always slightly overshadowed by a deep nostalgia for the era long gone.
As a teenager, Simone survived Nazi concentration camp where her parents and brother were murdered.

Both women prevailed despite having to confront and overcome unimaginable catalogue of life adversities. Both women could not possibly be more different, and at the same time, both have secured permanent place in my heart and mind.

But would I want to be one of them?

- *'These are great examples. If you could choose one of them, which one would it be?'* – comes the prompt…

'If I truly have to choose, well, I would like to be born always as **me**.'

They did not even pretend to hide their disappointment; it was all over their faces.
'I am quite happy being me, because…'

I was not given the chance to expand on my answer.

And yes, you guessed it, I did not get the job.

It was however a turning point in my life, because it made me realize that there must be some sort of justification behind these kind of questions.

There must be a general assumption that we are unhappy in our own skin and always either aspire to be someone else (mild case) or fantasize and pretend to be a person of our dreams (severe case).

Well, I am happy and content with who I am.

And I have just shocked the interviewing panel by admitting to such crime.

This book is the fruition of that interview.

'Know Thyself...'

'Know thyself' is one of my favorite aphorisms.

No other two words spell out in such concise way what is the essential element (the keystone if you like) of the foundation of happiness.

To 'know thyself' is to look deep into your soul and be able to display on the outside what is a mirror reflection of your inner self.

To 'know thyself' means having such deep understanding of who you really are that every single decision you make is automatically in harmony with what you truly desire.

To reach this level of self-awareness, you must analyze every aspect of your life and ask yourself; 'is this truly me or am I pretending to be someone else?'

You have to focus more on your internal thoughts, feelings and moods.

Only then, you will be able to master the elusive art of happiness.

Remember that it is never too late to change direction and start being yourself.

Artists do it all the time. Picasso did.

Not many people are aware of the fact, that Picasso, known for his cubism of course, started his artistic career with a strikingly realistic style. Just google 'View of the Port of Valencia' from 1895 or 'First Communion' from 1896 and you will understand.

Now look into the mirror of your soul and begin to 'know thyself'.

Notes

THE ART OF TAFELSPITZ – *BECAUSE YOU ARE WHAT YOU EAT*

In October 2016, I found myself in Vienna attending a clinical trial symposium. Our host, University of Vienna, have organized a dinner at the renowned Plachutta [2] restaurant and the main dish was Emperor's favorite – Tafelspitz.

It was my first time at this famous place, but it was not the first time I had Tafelspitz.

My memory went back to my childhood and my grandmother cooking this beef soup dish almost every Sunday. When I think of family dinners, I fondly recall my childhood and Tafelspitz.
Sitting there and staring at the food in front of me, I was both tearful and excited at the same time. I took photos of my dinner and I now call it my 'ratatouille [3] moment'.

So what does the Tafelspitz have to do with happiness?

Nothing and EVERYTHING at the same time.

Tafelspitz represents a traditional dish going back to the Austrian Empire, which is as popular today as it was during Emperor Frantz Joseph's reign. This simple dish is a testament to the ingenuity of local cuisine, and a lesson in how food can shape our wellbeing. We are literally, what we eat.

Few months later, I came across a very special book by anthropologist Stephen Le and was taken on a culinary journey to discover what a "100 Million Years of Food" [4] can teach us about happiness. How different food affects different people and why we should stick to eating traditional cuisine enjoyed by our ancestors.

The following arguments are especially convincing (emphasis added):

"In studies, traditional diets typically do at least as well as nutritionist-approved low-fat, low-salt diets in maintaining health. In part, this is because **the functions of dietary fat, cholesterol, and salt throughout the body are numerous**, while nutritionists have necessarily devoted their limited time and resources to narrow views on the harmful effects of these substances."

Mother Nature always gets it right after all.

Le explains further:

"Traditional eaters didn't bother with scientific studies; they cooked and combined food in ways that maximized their health. The older the cuisine, the better: Five-hundred-year-old-cuisines are a good starting point, because at that point industrially processed foods had not yet made significant inroads into people's diets".

"Traditional cuisines were moderate in fat, cholesterol, and/or salt and therefore tasted good; thus getting ourselves to stick with these diets in not difficult".

And this is why the Tafelspitz that my great-grandparents enjoyed circa 1900, is the same Tafelspitz I enjoy today.

I have to confess, I never thought about my dietary habits until I read Le's book.

I know believe that my good health is linked directly to what I eat.

I do not follow a specific diet and quite happily venture outside my 'comfort zone' while on holidays or out with friends and family. But I always come back to my staples, which is superbly simple and traditional food, once popular across the former Austro-Hungarian Empire.

What about you?

Your genes carry everything ever needed to process nutrients required to nourish your body.
You must however, deliver the right elements, not foreign objects in the form of various junk food.

If you are a vegetarian or a vegan, think what would your grandparents choose; a vegetable stew cooked from fresh produce you just picked up at a local market or a pre-packed gluey something advertised as 'vegan'... ✖

Start eating whole foods and avoid the processed stuff. **It can be your game changer!**

Notes

THE ART OF ENLIGHTENED MINIMALISM

"The question of what you want to own is really the question of how you want to live"

KonMarie

If owning a lot of stuff was any guarantor of happiness, Americans would be the happiest people in the world, and all wealthy people would be happy bunnies 24/7.

Except, that there is no such guarantee.

Sadly, our unhappiness is good for business. We become prime targets of collective advertising of all sorts. And when we feel under the weather, it is very easy to convince us to spend money on things we don't need, but buy anyway, in a mirage-d hope that we can buy happiness, if only for a day.

We end up with cluttered space and abundance of unwanted objects — what is widely recognized as both the symptoms and results of unhappiness.

It is time to de-clutter your life.

Do not worry, I am not going to propose that you get rid of most of your possessions and adhere to strict minimalism from now on.

I want to introduce you to a form of selective minimalism, with a strong emphasis on having just the right amount of everything.

I call it **Enlightened Minimalism.**

You may ask 'what exactly is the concept of enlightened minimalism'?

Well, it links directly to your inner image and projects this image into physical world in how you live, what you buy and even the way you dress.

It links directly to your inner self, because only you know what the right balance is when it comes to things that you want to surround yourself with.

As you develop an awareness of your true self, you will discover what the right amount of everything means for you.

Your home and your appearance will be a testament of the Art of Being You.

Clothes Speak Volume…

Clothes really do speak volume; therefore do not confuse your professional image with your private one.

Most of us have to get up each morning, get dressed and go to work.
You can take the stress out of getting dressed by creating a capsule wardrobe.

If you work five days a week, create five outfits per season – you will wear each outfit just about four times a month (in case you are worried about being seen wearing the same clothes).

Develop a consistent style of dress and always look professional, this will help you to convey self-confidence and make you feel invulnerable.

Find your signature item and wear it often. It can be something as simple as a souvenir bead bracelet from your favorite holiday.

Exercise **Joy-per-use** attitude.

Most people are familiar with the cost-per-use approach to justify their costlier than usual purchases.
I want to propose a fresher perspective so you can do something for your overall wellbeing – my concept of **JOY**-per-use attitude.

There are the weekends, holidays or just days off work – few more reasons to channel your inner self.

…And Your Home is Your Castle

It is time to instill some modern take on this proverbial expression.

We spend about a half of our entire life at home. Our home should be our fortress to which we gladly retrieve, which we enjoy and in which we find contentment.
Therefore, what is just the right amount of stuff at home in the context of our enlightened minimalism?

Which items should you keep?

What new things should you buy?

How much should you really de-clutter?

A study conducted by University College London found that looking at things, which we find beautiful makes us happy. **Start with those.**

When I walk into my living room, my eyes always rest on framed sheet of Beatrix Potter stamps, even if just for a few seconds. These are a very special gift from my son.

When I look up from my laptop screen right now, I see our family photo taken few years back during one of our most memorable holidays.

I have many framed photos, but I do not display them all at the same time. Too many items next to each other create a blurred wall of decorative wrongness. I like my favorite things to stand out, so they have to take turns being displayed.

Look around your home, room by room, wall by wall, and imagine your **ideal** home. Then act upon the image on the screen of your mind – keep all the things that make you feel happy, and get rid of things you do not want anymore. Make space for things you still plan to buy.

"Other people might want a Ferrari, but I wanted a butterfly house. I built it together with a blacksmith. We designed it together."

Andre Rieu

Notes

Notes

THE ART OF DOING NOTHING

"French women love to sit at a café and do nothing but enjoy the moment."

Mireille Guilliano

We live in a highly paced world, and our need to demonstrate to this world how busy we are is painstakingly clear from numerous social media posts:

'X is attending an event near you…'
'Y is travelling from… to…'
'Z is sleeping' – I have not actually seen this one yet, but it does not mean it is not out there.

We live in an era in which, if you do not have Facebook/twitter/Instagram account, you do not exist.
The fear of missing out is always present, so we keep posting and posting and updating and following.
Occasionally we are unnerved when we discover that our favorite influencers are being paid handsomely to promote things to us, but we also quickly forgive them and almost by default bounce back into 'following'.

Now, imagine that the World Wide Web is about to undergo a global maintenance and there will be no internet connection for a whole week.
Yes, no internet anywhere in the world for a week.

What would you do every day for 7 days?

Do you know yourself well enough to answer this question?

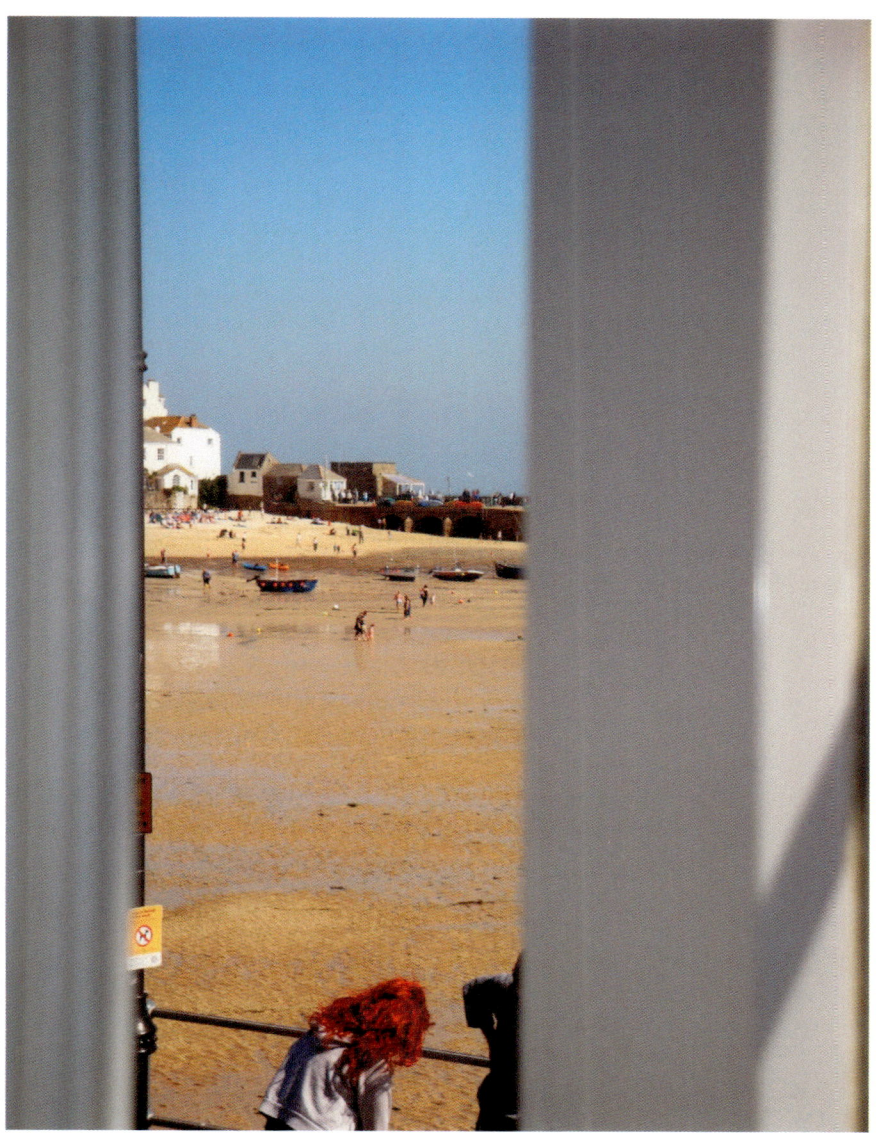

The Healing Art of Nature

I really hope that your answer to the question posted on the previous page would include spending more time in nature.

Spending time in nature offers undisputed benefits to both our mental and physical wellbeing.

A simple walk in the forest or park improves mood by reducing feelings of stress, anger or anxiety.

It is a place where we can turn our attention inwards and focus on our thoughts and feelings.

Nature is always there, and always ready to support us.

Spending time in nature is **essential if you are truly committed** to self-discovery and perfecting the art of happiness.
And it doesn't take much to create our private little green oasis…

How Does Your Garden Grow?

"We need to raise awareness of just how much gardens have to offer, how important they are to our quality of life.
They can offer physical health through getting people outdoors and active, spiritual wellbeing through the calm that a connection to nature brings, and cultural richness through their design and 'stories' that they tell.
And the best thing about these amazing assets?
As a resource, they are simply so accessible as they are all around us, from little window boxes, to pockets of greenery on street corners, to public parks to large visitor attraction gardens, we all have the opportunity to see and even make a garden."

Linden Groves [5]

PROTOCOL NOTES
THE ART OF BEING YOU – REVISITED

Knowledge is power.

And knowledge of your true self is the most powerful of all.

Each day, learn something new about yourself, so you can write **your own** 'Protocol of the Art of Happiness'.

The Timeless Touch of Chives

A day without fresh, finely chopped chives is a day when I'm on holidays and enjoying local cuisine. Unless of course chives are part of that cuisine.

For breakfast: I add chives to omelette, scrambled eggs or Viennese soft-boiled eggs.

For lunch: I sprinkle finely chopped chives on open face sandwiches, add them to tuna with mayo paste or any salad I fancy.

For dinner: Absolute must for any form of potatoes or to add a bit of flavor to soups – I use chives to garnish chicken of Tafelspitz beef soup.

The numerous health benefits of this humble herb are undisputable; chives are extremely rich in antioxidants, which help fight inflammation, colds and even cancer.

I eat them, because thanks to my grandmother, I love them!

The Art of Your Grandparents' Cuisine

BREAKFAST

The Art of Your Grandparents' Cuisine

LUNCH

The Art of Your Grandparents' Cuisine

DINNER

The Art of Your Grandparents' Cuisine

SNACK/SUPPER

YOU ARE WHAT YOU EAT NOTES

YOU ARE WHAT YOU EAT NOTES

Fundamentals of My Beige Minimalism

I am a self-certified beigeanatic since my clothes are mostly neutral colors of beige, white and navy blue, with beige claiming around 70% of my wardrobe.

Here are my thoughts on the fabulous beiges:

Best things in fashion come in beige: iconic Trench Coat, weekend chinos, Max Mara camel hair coat…
These classics are also planet-friendly; you can wear them today, tomorrow and in 10 years' time, as they never go out of style.

From oatmeal beige to taupe – there is a shade of beige for everyone.

For a clean summer look, pair beige with white.

Pair beige with black or navy for a chic autumn/winter look.

You can go beige head-to-toe, but avoid piling on too many things. Less is always more.

If you pair beige with color, let the color play a smaller part, otherwise your beige will 'disappear'.

Take good care of your beige handbags – it really is hard to keep them clean.

You can buy your favorite beige sweaters in twos and threes, just like you would buy your favorite white tee.

Beige looks good with jeans – Think Trench Coat and Jeans.

If you buy only one item in beige, let it be a Trench Coat. This truly classic piece will complement any outfit.

Fundamentals of **Your** Minimalism

Special Objects in **Your** Castle

How Does Your Garden Grow?

I love gardens, all of them - from the spectacular Rothschild gardens of the French Riviera, through my childhood memories of my grandmother's humble countryside rose garden, to inspiring English gardens I have the pleasure to visit these days.

I visit gardens and I collect books on gardens.

Linden Groves is the co-author of one of the most beautiful books on gardens: *'The Gardens of English Heritage'*.

The below transcript is a re-print from March 2015. It is as relevant today as it was over 5 years ago when I spoke to Linden about her magnificent book.

MP-S: The first thought that comes to mind while looking at the photos of gardens featured in your book is that... yes, human and nature can actually join forces and create something truly spectacular. The ingredients are always there, nature is abundant, but what can we do in today's computer dominated world to help people re-discover gardens? And I don't mean preserving nostalgia for the times long gone, but a genuine fascination that would produce new gardens for future generations to enjoy?

Linden Groves: *We need to raise awareness of just how much gardens have to offer, how important they are to our quality of life. They can offer physical health through getting people outdoors and active, spiritual wellbeing through the calm that a connection to nature brings and cultural richness through their design and the 'stories' that they tell. And the best thing about these amazing assets? As a resource, they are simply so accessible as they are all around us, from little window boxes, to pockets of greenery on street corners, to public parks to large visitor attraction gardens, we all have the opportunity to see and even make a garden. If we can get people to understand all this, then more value will be attached to producing new gardens, and caring for existing ones.*

MP-S: What is a quintessentially English garden? (and park?)

LG: *England has produced so many different types of garden, but the quintessential are probably the early 20th century gardens of Gertrude Jekyll and her admirers, in which colourful blooms spill over onto romantic pathways, framed with clipped evergreen hedges. But amongst those in the know, England also produced the highly-influential and much-loved landscape park of the 18th century, in which Capability Brown and his followers tore away the formal gardens of earlier periods and replaced them with sweeping grass rolling down slopes dotted with tree clumps and elegant garden buildings to serpentine lakes, creating gorgeous wide views. In 2016 we will all be celebrating the Tercentenary of Capability Brown's death and these fabulous landscapes will get the attention they deserve - www.capabilitybrown.org*

MP-S: You have probably heard this question many times before, but I have to ask: which is your favourite garden and why?

LG: *My favourite garden from the book is Wrest Park in Bedfordshire, England as it contains many different layers of landscape history, ranging from a striking 17th century* *ornamental canal to an 18th century bowling green, to Victorian parterres, to an almost-too-impressive 21st century playground! But the very best thing about Wrest is the survival of its 18th century formal woodland garden, which is very rare in this country, and offers a wonderful opportunity to stroll down long avenues and discover statuary hidden amongst the trees.*

MP-S: Did you always like outdoors as a child? How do you inspire your own children?

LG: *As a child, I always liked being in the freedom of outdoors and was also very romantic with a big imagination, and as historic gardens come with lots of amazing stories, I guess they enable me to indulge those childhood enthusiasms! I inspire my own children by never forcing them to be interested, but by giving them lots of opportunities to be outdoors if they would like. I like to think I tread a fine balance between not dumbing down, whilst always holding on to a love of silliness.*

MP-S: As a landscape/garden historian, would you ever consider writing a book about gardens of Europe? - That's just an example and 'Gardens of France' would be another one.

LG: *Gillian Mawrey, my co-author on the English Heritage book, is a great expert on the gardens of Europe, and in fact especially France. We originally met and became friends when I was her assistant at the Historic Gardens Foundation, an international charity which publishes a unique magazine, Historic Gardens Review, to bring together lovers of historic parks and gardens across the world. I certainly hope she produces a book on gardens of France soon, as it will be top of my Christmas list! www.historicgardens.org*

MP-S: Any projects currently under way?

LG: *I have just begun work on Experiencing Arcadia, which I am thrilled to be undertaking with a garden history partner-in-crime Dr Clare Hickman. This lovely project was inspired by our frustration that garden visitors today can sometimes be less like reliving the past and more like venturing into a museum. We want to know what it was like to walk around a garden in high-heeled 18th century shoes, or to actually have a banquet in a Banqueting House, so are exploring how digital resources can recapture some of this to give today's garden visitors an insight into the 18th century garden visiting experience, and sparking and inform fresh thinking amongst historic garden managers about new ways in which gardens can be made accessible for the public. http://www.outdoorchildren.co.uk/experiencing-arcadia/*

MP-S: Thank you.

Notes

The Art of You

Each day brings a new discovery…

Final Thoughts As You Start Writing Your Protocol:

Research The Art of Your Grandparents' Cuisine.

What would be your ancestors' typical breakfast, lunch, dinner or supper?

Define Fundamentals of Your Enlightened Minimalism.

Identify Special Objects in Your Castle.

Embrace occasional solitude so you can look into your soul and truly 'Know thyself'.

Make Nature Your Best Friend.

Remind yourself that happiness is an art, and **you are the Artist**.

Create Your Masterpiece!

Notes

Notes

Notes

Notes

Notes

Notes

Notes

References

The Art of Being You – The Most Important Kind of Art

[1] Simone Veil (1927 – 2017) – French politician and the first female president of the European Parliament from 1979 to 1983.

The Art of Tafelspitz

[2] PLACHUTTA WOLLZEILE

Wollzeile 38, 1010 Vienna, Austria

Phone: +43 1 512 15 77

[3] In Disney's cartoon 'Ratatouille', food critic Anton Ego tastes stewed vegetable dish ratatouille and is taken back in time to his childhood and his mother's delicious cooking. I refer to my Tafelspitz experience in 2016 as my 'ratatouille' moment.

[4] '100 Million Years of Food. What Our Ancestors Ate And Why It Matters Today' by Stephen Le

How Does Your Garden Grow?

[5] Linden Groves is the co-author of 'The Gardens of English Heritage'.

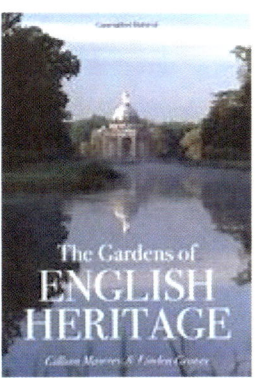

Meet the Author – The Introvert Me…